Jack C. Richards & C

Passages

Third Edition

Workbook 1 B

CAMBRIDGE
UNIVERSITY PRESS

CAMBRIDGE
UNIVERSITY PRESS

University Printing House, Cambridge CB2 8BS, United Kingdom

One Liberty Plaza, 20th Floor, New York, NY 10006, USA

477 Williamstown Road, Port Melbourne, VIC 3207, Australia

314–321, 3rd Floor, Plot 3, Splendor Forum, Jasola District Centre, New Delhi – 110025, India

79 Anson Road, #06–04/06, Singapore 079906

Cambridge University Press is part of the University of Cambridge.

It furthers the University's mission by disseminating knowledge in the pursuit of education, learning and research at the highest international levels of excellence.

www.cambridge.org
Information on this title: www.cambridge.org/9781107627208

© Cambridge University Press 2015

First published 1998
Second edition 2008
Third edition 2015
Update to Third edition published 2021

Printed in Great Britain by Ashford Colour Press Ltd.

A catalog record for this publication is available from the British Library

ISBN 978-1-009-04061-7 Student's Book 1 with eBook
ISBN 978-1-009-04076-1 Student's Book 1A with eBook
ISBN 978-1-009-04082-2 Student's Book 1A with eBook
ISBN 978-1-009-04086-0 Student's Book 1 with Digital Pack
ISBN 978-1-009-04087-7 Student's Book 1A with Digital Pack
ISBN 978-1-009-04088-4 Student's Book 1B with Digital Pack
ISBN 978-1-107-62725-3 Workbook 1
ISBN 978-1-107-62718-5 Workbook 1A
ISBN 978-1-107-62720-8 Workbook 1B
ISBN 978-1-107-62768-0 Teacher's Edition 1 with Assessment Audio
ISBN 978-1-107-62754-3 Class Audio 1
ISBN 978-1-009-04089-1 Full Contact 1 with Digital Pack
ISBN 978-1-009-04090-7 Full Contact 1A with Digital Pack
ISBN 978-1-009-04091-4 Full Contact 1B with Digital Pack
ISBN 978-1-107-62762-8 DVD 1
ISBN 978-1-107-66626-9 Presentation Plus 1

Additional resources for this publication at cambridgeone.org

Book design: Q2A / Bill Smith
Art direction, layout services and photo research: Tighe Publishing Services

Contents

Credits

Illustration credits

Kim Johnson: 4, 28, 45, 66, 67
Dan McGeehan: 7, 54
Paul Hostetler: 8, 27, 56, 60, 64
Koren Shadmi: 33, 52, 62
James Yamasaki: 22, 35, 61

Photography credits

1 ©Chris Bennett/Aurora/Getty Images; **3** (*clockwise from top center*) ©Keith Levit/Design Pics/Corbis, ©iStock/Thinkstock, ©Iconica/Commercial Eye/Getty Images; **6** ©Barry Austin Photography/Getty Images; **9** ©iStock/Thinkstock; **10** ©dieKleinert/Alamy; **11** ©Holger Hollemann/dpa/picture-alliance/Newscom; **12** ©Christian Guy/Getty Images; **13** ©iStock/Thinkstock; **14** ©iStock/Thinkstock; **15** ©iStock/Thinkstock; **16** ©John W Banagan/Photographer's Choice/Getty Images; **18** (*top left to right*) ©trekandshoot/Shutterstock, ©iStock/Thinkstock, ©iStock.com/wdstock, ©A. T. Willett/Alamy; (*bottom*) ©Rudolf Balasko/Thinkstock; **20** ©Media Bakery; **23** ©Blue Jean Images/Alamy; **24** ©andresrimaging/iStockphoto; **26** ©Pulp Photography/The Image Bank/Getty Images; **29** ©iStock/Thinkstock; **30** ©Clover/SuperStock; **31** ©Eric Isselee/Shutterstock; **34** ©Elke Meitzel/age fotostock; **36** (*top to bottom*) ©assalave/iStockphoto, ©Antonio Balaguer soler/Thinkstock; **38** ©iStock/Thinkstock; **40** ©Wavebreak Media/Thinkstock; **41** ©iStock.com/DSGpro; **44** (*left to right*) ©Jodi/Jake/Media Bakery, ©Masterfile Royalty Free, ©Andresr/age fotostock; **46** ©Caspar Benson/fstop/Corbis; **47** (*left to right*) ©wavebreakmedia/Shutterstock, ©Juanmonino/E+/Getty Images, ©iStock.com/pressureUA, ©homydesign/Shutterstock; **48** (*top*) Janos Levente/Shutterstock, (*center*) Sofi photo/Shutterstock; **49** ©Masterfile Royalty Free; **50** (*clockwise from top left*) Suprijono Suharjoto/Thinkstock, Blend Images/SuperStock, Jack Hollingsworth/Thinkstock, Jupiterimages/Thinkstock; **53** ©Mitchell Funk/Photographer's Choice/Getty Images; **56** ©Stockbyte/Thinkstock; **59** (*left to right*) ©Enrique Algarra/age fotostock, ©Dan Brownsword/Cultura/Getty Images, ©Masterfile Royalty Free; **63** ©Vicki Reid/E+/Getty Images; **68** ©Iakov Kalinin/Shutterstock; **70** Arvind Balaraman/Thinkstock; **71** (*left to right*) ©Greg Epperson/Shutterstock, ©Image Source/age fotostock; **Back cover:** (*clockwise from top*) ©Leszek Bogdewicz/Shutterstock, ©Wavebreak Media/Thinkstock, ©Blend Images/Alamy, ©limpido/Shutterstock

Text credits

The authors and publishers acknowledge the following sources of copyright material and are grateful for the permissions granted. While every effort has been made, it has not always been possible to identify the sources of all the material used, or to trace all copyright holders. If any omissions are brought to our notice, we will be happy to include the appropriate acknowledgments on reprinting.

48 Adapted from "Everyday Creativity," by Carlin Flora, *Psychology Today,* November 1, 2009. Psychology Today © Copyright 2005, www.Psychologytoday.com; **54** Adapted from "Why We Dream: Real Reasons Revealed," by Rachael Rettner, *LiveScience,* June 27, 2010. Reproduced with permission of LiveScience; **60** Adapted from "The Survival Guide for Dealing with Chronic Complainers," by Guy Winch, PhD, *Psychology Today*, July 15, 2011. Reproduced with permission of Guy Winch, www.guywinch.com; **66** Adapted from "Internet On, Inhibitions Off: Why We Tell All," by Matt Ridley, *The Wall Street Journal,* February 18, 2012. Reproduced with permission of The Wall Street Journal. Copyright © 2012 Dow Jones & Company, Inc. All Rights Reserved Worldwide; **72** Adapted from "International Careers: A World of Opportunity: Battling Culture Shock Starts with Trip to Local Bookstores, Seminars: Advance preparation is critical in adjusting to the challenges of life in a foreign country," by Karen E. Klein, *Los Angeles Times*, September 11, 1995. Copyright © 1995. Los Angeles Times. Reprinted with permission.

7 THE INFORMATION AGE

LESSON A ▶ *A weird, wired world*

1 VOCABULARY

Use the words and phrases in the box to complete the sentences.

app	the cloud	podcasts	text
blog	download	spyware	virus

1. This _____ *app* _____ lets me find the lowest price for gasoline from my phone.

2. Do you have Wi-Fi here? I need to _____ some files for work.

3. Now that I store everything in _____, I can access my data from anywhere.

4. If your device is running really slowly, it probably has a _____.

5. Cal writes opinion pieces about music and posts them on his _____.

6. Even though I moved abroad, I still listen to _____ of shows from my favorite hometown radio station online.

7. Many people find it's more convenient to _____ than to talk to people on the phone.

8. Some programs use _____ to gather private information without your knowledge.

2 GRAMMAR

One of the underlined words in each sentence is a mistake. Circle it and write the correct word in the blank.

1. In the near future, more cars will (been) driven by computers than by people. _____ *be* _____

2. More tablets are being using in the classroom all the time. _____

3. Medical data has going to be accessed online by both doctors and patients. _____

4. More songs have be downloaded this year than ever before. _____

5. All laptops in the store have being priced to sell quickly. _____

6. More and more TV shows having been made available through apps. _____

7. Increasingly, shopping and banking will be do on portable devices. _____

8. Smartphones are going to been designed with even more features. _____

VOCABULARY

Choose the connector that best completes each sentence.

1. Nat dropped his phone on the sidewalk yesterday. *Nevertheless /(As a result)*, it doesn't work anymore.

2. Parents should monitor the websites their children visit. *Additionally / On the other hand*, they need to talk to their children about Internet safety.

3. Cell phones are becoming more advanced. Some, *for instance / likewise*, have many of the capabilities of a computer.

4. Penny switched Internet service providers to save money. *Furthermore / In fact*, she's now spending $15 less each month.

5. I really don't like having a TV in my apartment. *Similarly / On the other hand*, it's useful to have one when I have friends over.

6. Higher education has become much more common due to technology. *For example / Therefore*, my cousin completed her degree online while living in another country.

GRAMMAR

Use the passive of the present continuous and your own information to complete the sentences.

1. Blogs *are being written by just about everybody these days!*

2. An increasing number of devices _____

3. Many online classes _____

4. Some spyware _____

5. More and more apps _____

WRITING

A Read the review of an online course. Underline and number the passages
where the author of the review does the following things.

1. names and explains the service
2. explains where the service is offered
3. mentions positive features
4. suggests how it could be improved
5. states who would find it useful and why

Saturday, August 10

Curious about app creation?

Creating Mobile Apps is an online course that gives students the chance to explore a variety of app-building programs, to learn about the various uses of apps, and to develop their own app. Offered by Kelly Community College, it's an excellent source of information and hands-on experience for beginners while providing exposure to the latest programs for those who already have some experience.

As someone already familiar with building apps, I was not very impressed with some of the material. However, I found the section on the possible uses of apps for everything – from shopping to home security – really eye-opening. Additionally, being able to create an app under the guidance of an expert made the whole process seem much simpler than expected. Overall, it provided a flexible learning experience, and I found that the biggest advantage of an online class is that you can move at your own pace. On the other hand, there's the obvious lack of real time spent with the instructor and fellow students.

I would definitely recommend this course to anyone looking to build an app. My only suggestion is that the college should offer better networking tools so that the discussions and brainstorming sessions are more efficient.

B Use one of these topics or your own idea to write a product or service review.

• a course you took   • a social networking site   • software you tried

_____

_____

_____

_____

_____

_____

_____

_____

_____

_____

LESSON B ▶ *Information overload*

1 VOCABULARY

Use the words and phrases in the box to complete the sentences.

banner ads	bumper sticker	infomercial	spam	text messages
billboard	crawl	pop-up ads	telemarketing	voice mail

1. Have you seen that funny ad for a tablet on a huge _____*billboard*_____ on the highway?

2. A(n) _____ is a long commercial that looks like a TV show.

3. I'm not sure how effective _____ is. I never answer calls from numbers I don't recognize.

4. The _____ at the bottom of the TV screen said a storm was coming.

5. If I don't answer my phone, just leave me a _____.

6. I rarely see _____ on my computer because my browser blocks them really well.

7. I find _____ really annoying when they appear everywhere on a blog I'm reading.

8. All _____ email I receive is sent to a separate folder that gets automatically cleared once a week.

9. I'm uncomfortable talking on my phone in public, so I prefer to send _____.

10. The car in front of me had a _____ that said, "I'm not driving too fast – I sure hope you aren't!"

2 GRAMMAR

Complete these negative questions or tag questions with *doesn't, don't, isn't, shouldn't,* or *wouldn't.*

1. __*Don't*_____ you think that there are lots of great cooking sites online?

2. _____ it be terrific if Wi-Fi were free for everyone?

3. Sam's probably in a meeting. It's better to leave him a voice mail, _____ it?

4. _____ Sheila register for classes online before they fill up?

5. _____ it seem like it's impossible to keep up with your social networking accounts at times?

6. Computer viruses are getting more sophisticated, _____ you think?

7. _____ it strange that no one has sent me any email today?

8. Banner ads get really annoying when they take up too much of the screen, _____ they?

GRAMMAR

Rewrite the sentences in two ways using negative questions and tag questions and the words in parentheses.

1. It's amazing how much time someone can waste online. (isn't)

   Isn't it amazing how much time someone can waste online?

   It's amazing how much time someone can waste online, isn't it?

2. It would be great to get a bus wrap to advertise our business. (wouldn't)

   _____

   _____

3. Students should try to avoid sending text messages during class. (shouldn't)

   _____

   _____

4. It seems like new technologies are being invented every day. (doesn't)

   _____

   _____

5. It's annoying that some ads move all over the computer screen. (isn't)

   _____

   _____

6. It's amazing how some people can watch infomercials for hours. (don't you think)

   _____

   _____

GRAMMAR

Write negative questions or tag questions about things you can do online.
Choose from the items in the box or use your own ideas.

shopping
reading the news
watching videos
planning a vacation
making new friends
looking for a job

1. *It's so convenient to shop online nowadays, isn't it?* _____

2. _____

3. _____

4. _____

5. _____

6. _____

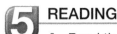

5 READING

A Read the blog post. Find the boldfaced words that match these definitions.

1. prepared; having no objection ___willing___
2. someone you know, but not well _____
3. invited to connect on a social network _____
4. accidents _____
5. are grateful for _____
6. at the same time _____

Are You **Tech** Obsessed?

Most of us **appreciate** the convenience of our tech devices, but for some people, it goes beyond a healthy appreciation. Take this quiz about tech obsession. How many of these are true for you?

1. Do you ever have **mishaps** because you are using your device while walking?

2. Are you **willing** to wait in line for more than 12 hours to get the latest version of a device?

3. Do you wake up in the middle of the night to check all your social networking accounts?

4. Do you text your friends even when they are in the same room?

5. Do you ever watch different shows on your phone, tablet, and TV **simultaneously**?

6. Do you check your phone continuously when you're out with friends or family at a movie, a sporting event, or a restaurant?

7. Do you change your device covers all the time? Are you one of the millions who love choosing new "fashions" for their devices?

8. Do you use online slang when you're offline? For example, you might say about a new **acquaintance**, "I **friended** him in English class last week."

This quiz was pretty funny, don't you think? Unfortunately, I answered "yes" to seven of the questions! How about you? Are you tech obsessed like me?

Posted by Walker White at 5:36 p.m.

B Read the statements. Do you think the author of the blog post would say these behaviors are obsessive or not obsessive? Choose the correct answer.

	Obsessive	Not obsessive
1. You have to be reminded to check your device for calls and messages.	☐	☑
2. People don't always understand you because you use a lot of online slang.	☐	☐
3. You often trip and fall in the street because you're checking email on your phone.	☐	☐
4. You have been using the same version of your device for several years.	☐	☐
5. You have a huge collection of colorful covers for your devices.	☐	☐
6. You turn off your device when you're with friends.	☐	☐

8 PUTTING THE MIND TO WORK

LESSON A ▶ *Exploring creativity*

1 GRAMMAR

Rewrite the sentences by making the reduced clauses into full clauses.

1. A person with great cooking and business skills would make a good restaurant owner.
   A person who has great cooking and business skills would make a
   good restaurant owner.

2. Those able to think creatively are the best team leaders.
   _____

3. A person opening a new business should try unusual marketing methods.
   _____

4. People with musical skills should share their talent with others.
   _____

5. People hoping to succeed in the arts should be prepared for financial challenges.
   _____

2 GRAMMAR

Reduce each relative clause. Then complete the sentences with your own ideas.

1. A person who is living on a tight budget . . .
   A person living on a tight budget shouldn't eat out too often.

2. Anyone who is interested in becoming a doctor . . .
   _____

3. Someone who is considering an artistic career . . .
   _____

4. People who are able to work at home . . .
   _____

5. A supervisor who has too much work to do . . .
   _____

6. A person who is required to take a foreign language in school . . .
   _____

7. People who are becoming bored with their jobs . . .
   _____

3 VOCABULARY

A Write the nouns that relate to the adjectives.

1. curious _____curiosity_____
2. decisive _____
3. determined _____
4. disciplined _____
5. innovative _____
6. knowledgeable _____
7. motivated _____
8. original _____
9. passionate _____
10. patient _____
11. perceptive _____
12. resourceful _____

B Now write sentences about these people using adjectives and nouns from above.

1. business executive _A knowledgeable person who has innovative ideas_
   might make a good business executive.

2. web designer _____
   _____

3. journalist _____
   _____

4. lawyer _____
   _____

4 GRAMMAR

What qualities are needed to do these jobs? Use reduced relative clauses in your answers.

singer

landscaper

architect

1. _A person considering_
   becoming a singer needs
   _to be_ _____
   _____
   _____

2. _____
   _____
   _____
   _____

3. _____
   _____
   _____
   _____

WRITING

A Read Erica's story. Choose the word or words you would use to describe her.

☐ curious ☐ determined ☐ original ☐ resourceful

If you've ever planned a big event, something like this may have happened to you, but I certainly never thought it would happen to me! My fiancé and I were planning to get married in six months when his company decided to transfer him overseas – in two weeks! He wouldn't be able to return to the U.S. for some time, which meant we couldn't get married as planned. I told a friend about this, and she said, "So get married now!" I reminded her that there was no time to plan anything. She responded, "Then get creative." So I did. First, I designed and sent out email invitations. Then, as there was no time to book a venue, we decided to have both the ceremony and reception in my parents' backyard. My mother put together the decorations, which were flowering plants in pots. A friend of mine who's a chef prepared the food, and we had lots of cupcakes instead of a big cake. The clothes were the biggest challenge; there wasn't any time to make a new dress as I had planned. Luckily, I remembered the dress I'd made for a project in college. With a few alterations, it was perfect. I asked my three bridesmaids to wear dresses they already had – in any color. In the end, the wedding was fantastic thanks to everyone putting their creativity to work.

B Read the story again. Write a *P* where you think each new paragraph should begin.

C Write a three-paragraph composition about a problem you actually had or imagine you might have. How did you or would you solve the problem?

    If you _____, something like this may have happened to you,

but I certainly never thought it would happen to me. _____

_____

_____

_____

_____

_____

_____

_____

_____

1 VOCABULARY

Choose the word that best completes each sentence.

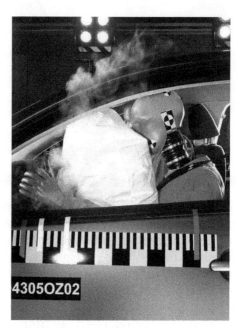

43050Z02

1. Seat belts alone did not protect car passengers enough, which is why researchers (found) / made / solved a safer solution: air bags for cars.

2. You need to *explore / organize / solve* your information before you present it to other people. Otherwise, they won't understand it.

3. Our report *explored / made / solved* several possibilities for increasing the car's efficiency.

4. The board of directors *analyzed / found / organized* the alternatives carefully when they chose a new location for the research facility.

5. It's important to consider many solutions when you are *making / organizing / solving* a problem.

6. Our science experiment didn't work. We *explored / made / solved* a mistake in the calculations.

2 GRAMMAR

Read the conversation. Find the mistakes in the underlined sentences, and rewrite them so that they are correct. The mistake might be use of commas.

A: Why are we leaving so early? The meeting doesn't start for another 30 minutes!

B: At this time of day, the traffic is terrible! (1) It moves at only about 20 miles an hour, that means we need to leave now.

A: Why don't we take public transportation?

B: (2) The buses are even slower which is why people avoid using them.

A: Then how about walking? (3) The office is a short distance from here, which it means that it shouldn't take long.

B: True. (4) And we can get some exercise, too, it is great!

1. *It moves at only about 20 miles an hour, which means (that) we need to leave now.*
   _____

2. _____
   _____

3. _____
   _____

4. _____
   _____

3 GRAMMAR

Write sentences about these topics. Use non-defining relative clauses beginning with
which is why or *which means (that)*.

the common cold   *ATM*   *video chatting*   *pollution*

1. There is no cure for the common cold, *which is why researchers are working to*
   find one.

2. ATMs are available everywhere, _____

3. Video chatting is easy for almost everyone, _____

4. Pollution has become less of a problem in many cities, _____

4 GRAMMAR

Combine the sentences with non-defining relative clauses beginning with *which is why,*
which means (that), or *which is* + adjective.

1. People feel the need to keep in touch. Social networking sites are popular.
   People feel the need to keep in touch, which is why social networking sites
   are popular.

2. New diseases are being discovered all the time. Researchers have to work even harder.
   _____

3. Some people like listening to music on vinyl records. It's strange to me.
   _____

4. Traffic congestion is becoming a major problem in cities. New types of public
   transportation will have to be developed.
   _____

5. Reality TV shows are cheap and easy to produce. There are so many of them now.
   _____

5 READING

A Read the article quickly. Choose the best title for the article.

☐ Some People Will Never Be Creative   ☐ How to Become an Artist

☐ What Everyday Creativity Means

When we think of creativity, we think of Mozart, Picasso, Einstein – people with a combination of talent and opportunity. But the truth is that all sorts of people are capable of engaging in creative processes. Just because you don't plan to be a famous actor or choreographer doesn't mean that you can't use your natural creativity and make your life your own masterpiece.

Zorana Ivcevic, a psychologist who studies creativity, has found that while some people fit into more traditional creative roles, as dancers or scientists, many others express their creativity through more routine acts. She also found that certain personality traits are shared by the "officially" creative and those who practice everyday creativity. Both groups tend to be open-minded and curious, and they are persistent, positive, energetic, and motivated by their chosen activities. And while 30 percent of the people studied showed no signs of creativity, they shouldn't lose hope. Other studies show that taking up creative pursuits actually makes people more flexible and less judgmental.

Experts at the Harvard Medical School define everyday creativity as expressions of originality and meaningfulness. Rebecca Whitlinger provided an example of this when she decided to make use of her seemingly useless collection of bridesmaid dresses. She resolved to wear them everywhere and asked friends to take snapshots of her wearing them in many unlikely situations, even while parasailing. Then it occurred to her to turn this idea into a fundraising event for a charity she worked for. Guests were asked to wear outfits they would be unable to wear again (such as a bridesmaid dress). Creative? Yes. Meaningful? Well, the fundraiser made $90,000 in its first few years.

"It's too bad that, when considering what endeavors may be creative, people immediately think of the arts," says Michele Root-Bernstein, co-author of *Sparks of Genius*. "It's the problem-solving processes they exhibit rather than the content or craft that make them so. Just about anything we do can be addressed in a creative manner, from housecleaning to personal hobbies to work."

B Read the article again. Choose the answers that best reflect the ideas in the article.

1. According to Zorana Ivcevic, how many people naturally show signs of creativity?

    ☐ a. everyone   ☐ b. more people than most of us think   ☐ c. very few people

2. According to the article, which of these personality traits is not as commonly linked to creativity?

    ☐ a. impatience   ☐ b. optimism   ☐ c. curiosity

3. Rebecca Whitlinger had the idea for a fundraising event when she . . .

    ☐ a. joined a charity.   ☐ b. took up photography.   ☐ c. creatively reused some clothes.

4. Michele Root-Bernstein believes that creativity can be . . .

    ☐ a. found in everything we do.   ☐ b. found only in the arts.   ☐ c. hard to define.

9 GENERALLY SPEAKING

LESSON A ▶ *How typical are you?*

1 GRAMMAR

Choose the expression that best completes each sentence.

1. (*Unlike*) / *While* many Americans, people in my country do not watch a lot of TV.
2. *In contrast to* / *While* many of my friends eat meat, I'm a vegetarian.
3. Monica is a typical teenager, *unlike* / *except for the fact that* she likes to get up early in the morning.
4. *Unlike* / *While* lots of my friends, I spend very little time on my phone.
5. I'm similar to people my age, *while* / *except that* I don't live at home.
6. *Unlike* / *While* most of my classmates, I prefer walking home to taking the bus.
7. Students in my country are just like other teens, *unlike* / *except that* we sometimes have to go to school on Saturdays.
8. I like all kinds of music, *except that* / *except for* jazz.

2 VOCABULARY

Use the words and phrases in the box to complete the sentences.

amenable
conform to
conservative
fits in
follows the crowd
make waves
rebellious
unconventional

1. Emma _____*fits in*_____ easily with the other girls in her college.
2. I don't mind working overtime. I'm actually quite _____ to it.
3. Neil likes to do his own thing. He doesn't _____ other people's ideas.
4. Sam does the opposite of what people tell him to do. He's very _____.
5. My town is very resistant to change. It's quite _____.
6. Sadie always goes along with her friends' plans. She doesn't like to _____.
7. Jake has _____ ideas about his work. He tries to be original.
8. My cousin usually _____ when it comes to fashion. She likes to dress exactly like her friends.

3 GRAMMAR

Read these descriptions of people. Who are you similar to or different from? Write sentences using *unlike, while, in contrast to, except that, except for,* and *except for the fact that.*

What are you like ?

I am a college sophomore, and my major is English literature. My interests include tennis, reading, and travel. I enjoy exploring new places – especially places few people visit.
—KIM

Hi! I love music of all kinds, and I play guitar in a band. I love loud music – the louder the better. I'm interested in musical instruments, and I enjoy collecting them.
—MARIA

I am a 25-year-old computer science student. I am very interested in technology and soccer. I love building computers in my spare time.
—DONALD

Do you like visiting historical sites? Do you enjoy reading books about history? I do. I am 23 and an accountant, but my real passion is history. I also enjoy collecting rare coins.
—LUIS

1. *I have a lot in common with Kim, except that I don't like sports.*

2. _____

3. _____

4. _____

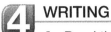

WRITING

A Read these paragraphs and answer the questions.

More and more Americans are living alone nowadays. While an increasing number of people end up living alone because of varying life circumstances, such as a change in marital status, more people are choosing to live alone today than in the past. According to a recent U.S. census, 28 percent of all households in the United States are made up of just one person. This is a dramatic change from the extended families of just a couple of generations ago.

1. What is the topic sentence?

_____

2. What reasons are given to support the topic sentence?

_____

_____

3. What fact is given to support the topic sentence?

_____

The typical American living alone is neither old nor lonely. In fact, about 5 million people between the ages of 18 and 34 live alone, and the majority of them have chosen to do so. They are acting on a desire to be more independent, and they often have a more varied social life.

4. What is the topic sentence?

_____

5. What fact is given to support the topic sentence?

_____

6. What reasons are given to support the topic sentence?

_____

_____

B Choose the topic sentence below that you like best. Then add at least four supporting statements to make a complete paragraph.

- It is *unusual / typical* for young people in my country to live alone.
- It is *easy / difficult* to get into college in my country.

_____

_____

_____

_____

_____

_____

1 GRAMMAR

Complete the blog post with *used to* or *would* and the words in the box. Sometimes more than one answer is possible.

like	listen	not be	not turn on	play	save	watch

http://blogs.cup.org/ryansreflections

Sunday, March 14

I had a funny conversation with my grandfather the other day. He was telling me what things were like when he was a kid. First of all, there (1) ____*didn't use to be*____ any technology like tablets, smartphones, or handheld game consoles to entertain him. When he wanted to hear music, he (2) _____ to the radio, or he (3) _____ a record on a record player. He did have a TV, but he (4) _____ it only at night. He (5) _____ the TV during the day because there were only four channels, and the programs were boring in the daytime. He also said he (6) _____ reading mystery and suspense novels. He (7) _____ his allowance to buy his favorite books. I feel kind of bad for my granddad – it doesn't sound like the most exciting childhood.

2 VOCABULARY

Complete the conversation with *keep* or *stay*. Sometimes more than one answer is possible.

Lola: Mrs. Wu's class is so difficult! I'm always up late studying for her class, so I can barely (1) ____*stay*____ awake the next morning. I don't know how I'll survive the semester!

Max: Yeah, I remember how demanding Mrs. Wu can be. My best advice is to (2) _____ up with the work you need to do each day. And don't procrastinate!

Lola: That's good advice. Her assignments are long and complicated. I always worry I won't be able to (3) _____ my grades up in her class!

Max: Even though you're stressed out, try to (4) _____ things in perspective. Also, if you let her know that you'll do what it takes to get good grades, maybe she'll help you (5) _____ out of trouble.

Lola: That's a good idea. I'll talk to Mrs. Wu tomorrow. And I'll (6) _____ in touch with you to let you know how things go.

3 GRAMMAR

Rewrite each sentence using the past habitual with *used to* or *would*. If there are two possibilities, write them both.

1. James was a very good chess player when he was younger.
   James used to be a very good chess player when he was younger.

2. In college, my friends and I studied for our tests together at the library.

   _____

3. I always asked my older sister for help with my science homework.

   _____

4. My English teacher didn't assign work over holidays or long weekends.

   _____

5. Rowan lived in an apartment near the university.

   _____

6. Carrie emailed her mom every day when she went away to school.

   _____

4 GRAMMAR

Complete the sentences with *used to* or *would* and information that is true for you.

1. Three years ago, I _____*used to*_____ live
   in a very noisy apartment on a noisy
   city street.

2. Last summer, my friends and I _____

   _____

   _____

3. When I was younger, I _____ go to

   _____

   _____

   _____

4. A friend of mine _____ have trouble in _____
   class because _____

5. My favorite teacher was _____. He/She _____

   _____

6. When I was first learning English, I _____

   _____

A Read the article quickly. What is Deirdre Barrett's main theory on dreaming?

YOUR **DREAMS** CAN HELP SOLVE YOUR DAY'S **PROBLEMS**

The slumbering mind might not seem like the best tool for critical thinking, but according to recent research, humans can actually solve problems while asleep. In fact, one purpose for dreaming may be to help us find solutions to puzzles that bother us while we're awake. Dreams are highly visual and often illogical, which makes them useful for the type of "out-of-the-box" thinking that some problem solving requires, explained Deirdre Barrett, a psychologist at Harvard University. Barrett's theory on dreaming boils down to this: Dreaming is really just thinking, but in a slightly different state from when our eyes are open.

Barrett has studied problem solving in dreams for more than 10 years and has documented many examples of the phenomenon in this time. In one experiment, Barrett asked college students to pick a homework problem to try to solve while sleeping. Students focused on the problem each night before they went to bed. At the end of a week, about half of the students had dreamed about the problem, and about a quarter had had a dream that contained the answer.

Having extensively reviewed scientific and historical literature for examples of problems solved in dreams, Barrett also found almost every type of problem being solved, from the mathematical to the artistic. Many were problems that required the individual to visualize something in his or her mind, such as an inventor picturing a new device. The other major category of problems solved included "ones where the conventional wisdom is just wrong about how to approach the problem," Barrett said. She added that dreams might have developed to be particularly good at allowing us to work out puzzles that fall into these two categories. "It's just extra thinking time," she stressed – though it's time that allows us to think in more flexible and creative ways.

$e = mc^2$ $dS \geq 0$ $a^2 + b^2 = c^2$ $\pi = c/d$

B Read the article again. Are the statements true or false? Choose the correct answer. Then rewrite the false statements to make them true.

	True	False
1. The creative thinking associated with dreams makes them good for some types of problem solving.	☐	☐
2. Barrett has only recently begun studying dreams.	☐	☐
3. The students in Barrett's experiment all solved their problems while asleep.	☐	☐
4. According to Barrett, only certain kinds of problems can be solved while dreaming.	☐	☐
5. Inventors may find dreams particularly useful.	☐	☐

1 GRAMMAR

Use the clauses in the box to complete the sentences.

how quickly the battery runs down   when my favorite show is interrupted by a news bulletin
people who make noise when they eat   who honk their horns all the time
waiting a long time to be seated   why people push in front of me in line
water dripping in the sink

1. The thing that really bothers me at the dinner table is . . .

   The thing that really bothers me at the dinner table is people who make noise when they eat.

2. When I'm trying to sleep at night, something that irks me is . . .

   _____

3. One thing I can't understand in the supermarket is . . .

   _____

4. The thing that really irritates me when I go to a restaurant is . . .

   _____

5. Something I can't stand is drivers . . .

   _____

6. Something that bothers me about my new cell phone is . . .

   _____

7. When I'm watching TV, one thing that bugs me is . . .

   _____

2 GRAMMAR

Write sentences about things that irritate you. Use relative clauses and noun clauses, and your own ideas.

1. *The thing that bothers me at the dinner table is when people talk with their mouths full.*

2. _____

   _____

3. _____

   _____

4. _____

   _____

3 GRAMMAR

Use relative clauses and noun clauses to write about everyday annoyances in these places.

on the road   **in the park**   **in the library**   **on the subway**

1. *The thing that annoys me on the road is when other drivers follow too closely.*

2. _____

3. _____

4. _____

4 VOCABULARY

Choose the word that best completes each sentence. Sometimes more than one answer is possible.

1. One thing that *drives /(gets)/ makes* me down is when it rains on the weekend.

2. Something that *drives / gets / makes* me up the wall is when I have to wait on a long line to buy one or two items.

3. The thing that *drives / gets / makes* my blood boil is when my sister borrows my clothes.

4. One thing that *drives / gets / makes* me upset is when people are rude to store clerks for no reason.

5. The one thing that *drives / gets / makes* under my skin is when someone's cell phone rings during a movie or play.

6. When I'm talking to someone, the thing that *drives / gets / makes* on my nerves is when he or she keeps interrupting me.

7. My sister sending text messages during dinner *drives / gets / makes* me crazy.

8. One thing my brother does that *drives / gets / makes* me sick is when he leaves piles of dirty dishes in the kitchen sink.

A Read the email complaining about a service. Number the four paragraphs in a logical order.

To: customerservice@bestgym.cup.com

Subject: Complaint about personal training service

To whom it may concern:

My trainer, Dan, has not arrived on time for a single 6:00 a.m. session. The earliest he has arrived is 6:15, and several times he has come at 6:30. I am paying extra for his services, and I am certainly not getting my money's worth. Dan also tends to wander off while I am exercising, getting involved in conversations with other gym employees. My understanding was that he would carefully supervise my training, which he has not done.

When I signed up for the program, the head trainer and I sat down, discussed my problems and needs, and drew up a plan, which was signed by both of us. This will show clearly what my expectations were in case you need to see this in writing. However, I hope it's clear by now that my needs have not been met.

I would like you to assign me a new trainer or refund my fee for the personal training service. If you can't do this by next week, I will take my business to another gym.

I am writing to complain about the personal trainer who was recently assigned to me at your gym. I signed up for six weeks of the intensive training program, including an individual fitness evaluation, and I am extremely dissatisfied.

Sincerely,
Elizabeth Smith
212-555-0199

B Use the numbers you wrote for the paragraphs above to answer these questions. In which paragraph does the writer . . .

a. explain the problem in detail? _____

b. explain what she wants? _____

c. describe the type of service clearly? _____

d. mention evidence of a service contract? _____

C Write an email complaining about a problem regarding a service or product you are not satisfied with.

To whom it may concern:

_____

_____

_____

_____

_____

_____

_____

LESSON B ► *Let's do something about it!*

GRAMMAR

Write *S* for a simple indirect question and *C* for a complex indirect question.

  <u>S</u> 1. I want to find out how to use less fat in my cooking.

____ 2. Why people aren't concerned about the crime rate is a mystery to me.

____ 3. I wonder if other people are concerned about the pollution problems in our city.

____ 4. The thing I don't get is why food prices are so high.

____ 5. One of my concerns is whether I will be able to afford a new car.

____ 6. I'd like to know if the weather will be nice this weekend.

____ 7. How some people can listen to such loud music is something I can't understand.

____ 8. I want to know when a cure for the common cold will be discovered.

GRAMMAR

Use the phrases in parentheses to rewrite the questions.

1. Why are the trains running so slowly? (. . . is a mystery to me.)
   <u>*Why the trains are running so slowly is a mystery to me.*</u>

2. Will there be cheaper health care for employees? (One of my concerns . . .)
   _____

3. Why do I get so much junk mail? (. . . is something I can't understand.)
   _____

4. How can you eat so much and not feel sick? (What I don't get . . .)
   _____

5. Who should I call if I don't get my passport on time? (I wonder . . .)
   _____

6. Will politicians do more to help the environment? (I'd like to know . . .)
   _____

7. Why don't people turn off their cell phones when they're at the movies?
   (. . . is beyond me.)
   _____

8. Why can't James get to work on time? (. . . is the thing that concerns me.)
   _____

9. Why do I get a cold every summer? (. . . is a mystery to me.)
   _____

10. Did someone use my tablet while I was out of the room? (I want to find out . . .)
   _____

VOCABULARY

Choose the word that best completes each sentence.

1. Lena was (infuriated)/ insulted when she missed her flight due to the traffic jam.

2. John was very *irritated / saddened* to hear about the house that had been damaged by the storm.

3. Vicky was *depressed / mystified* when the forecast called for rain on her wedding day.

4. The players on the football team were *humiliated / insulted* when they lost the championship game by 22 points.

5. We were absolutely *demoralized / stunned* when we found out we had won the prize.

6. Chiang was totally *baffled / discouraged* when a complete stranger started talking to him as if they were old friends.

7. Joan was *enraged / discouraged* when she saw that someone had damaged her car and not even left a note for her.

8. June became pretty *insulted / annoyed* when her Wi-Fi kept disconnecting.

GRAMMAR

Write sentences about each urban problem below or about ideas of your own.

transportation	sanitation	parking

1. I don't know *why bus service is so infrequent. It's almost impossible*
   to get to work on time.

2. It's beyond me _____

_____

3. I wonder _____

_____

4. My big concern _____

_____

A Read the article quickly. Write the number of each section next to its title.

_____ a. Understanding What Chronic Complainers Want

_____ b. Understanding What Chronic Complainers Don't Want

_____ c. Understanding How Chronic Complainers Think

The Survival Guide For Dealing With Chronic Complainers

*Optimists see a glass half full. Pessimists see a glass half empty. Chronic complainers see a glass that is slightly **chipped**, holding water that isn't cold enough, probably because it's tap water when they asked for bottled.*

The constant negativity of chronic complainers presents a challenge for those around them. Trying to remain positive and productive when there's a constant stream of complaints can try anyone's patience. And trying to be helpful will only **backfire**. So here are some essential tips to help those who deal with chronic complainers on a daily basis.

1 Despite the **gloom**, complainers don't see themselves as negative people. They see *the world* as negative and themselves as responding to the unfortunate circumstances of their lives.

Survival Tip #1 Never try to convince complainers that things are "not as bad" as they seem. This will only encourage them to come up with 10 additional **misfortunes** that might help you understand how terrible their lives actually are.

2 Chronic complainers are looking for sympathy and emotional **validation**. All they really want is for you to tell them that, yes, they've gotten a bad deal, and you feel their pain – just not as much as they do.

Survival Tip #2 The quickest way to get away from a complainer is to express sympathy and then change the subject. For example, "The printer jammed on you again? Sorry! I know it's hard, but I hope you can be a trooper because we really have to get back to work."

3 The idea that chronic complainers' lives are filled with tragedy is a big part of their **sense of identity**. Therefore, even good advice is a threat, because what complainers really want is for you to know they are suffering. They will often tell you why your solution won't work or might even become upset because you don't understand how unsolvable their problems are.

Survival Tip #3 You should avoid offering advice or solutions and stick to sympathy. However, there are situations where a problem is obviously very real. In this case, offer sympathy followed by brief but clear advice, and it will probably be accepted and appreciated.

B Read the article. Find the boldfaced word that matches each definition.

1. lack of hope ___*gloom*___

2. bad things that happen _____

3. your idea of who you are _____

4. have the opposite effect to what was intended _____

5. damaged because a small piece has broken off _____

6. proof that something is true or real _____

1 GRAMMAR

Complete the sentences with *even if, only if,* or *unless.*

1. I wouldn't interrupt a lesson _____*unless*_____ I had an important question.

2. I would leave the scene of a car accident _____ I knew for sure that no one was injured.

3. _____ I were really hungry, I still wouldn't take food that wasn't mine.

4. I would ask my neighbors to be more quiet in the morning _____ we had a good relationship.

5. I wouldn't ask to borrow a friend's phone _____ I knew he or she wouldn't mind.

6. _____ I didn't like my brother's new wife, I'd still be nice to her.

2 VOCABULARY

Choose the correct words to complete the sentences.

1. Steph won't mind if we rewrite parts of her article. She's very (agreeable) / *rational* to change.

2. It's *disapproving / unfair* that Mrs. Moore only blamed Lydia for the accident. Terry was responsible for the accident, too.

3. I'm sure Mark wasn't being *honest / irresponsible* when he said he liked my new shoes.

4. I can't believe Brianna wasn't fired from her job. Her *trustworthy / unscrupulous* business practices have cost this company thousands of dollars.

5. Min-hee is a good choice for club treasurer. She's good with money, and she's quite *unethical / responsible*.

6. In many places, it's *illegal / logical* to use a cell phone and drive at the same time.

3 GRAMMAR

Respond to what the first speaker says in each of these conversations.

1. A: If I found a friend's diary, I'd read it.

   B: Really? I wouldn't read it, even if <u>*I were*</u>
      <u>*really curious, because diaries are*</u>
      <u>*supposed to be private.*</u>

2. A: You should never give a friend your email password.

   B: I would give a friend my email password only if _____

      _____

3. A: If I heard someone spreading false information about a good friend, I wouldn't tell that friend about it.

   B: I wouldn't tell my friend about the false information unless _____

      _____

4. A: I would lend my best friend money if she needed it.

   B: I wouldn't lend my best friend a lot of money unless _____

      _____

4 GRAMMAR

How do you feel about these situations? Write sentences about them using *unless*, *only if*, or *even if*.

- recommending a friend's restaurant you don't consider very good
- lending money to someone you barely know
- giving fashion advice to a friend whose clothes you consider inappropriate
- saying you like a gift that you really don't like just to be nice

1. <u>*I would never recommend a friend's restaurant that I don't consider very good*</u>
   <u>*unless I knew he/she was trying to improve it.*</u>

2. _____

   _____

3. _____

   _____

4. _____

   _____

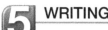

WRITING

A Read this composition and choose the best thesis statement.

- ☐ I am glad that I learned the importance of being responsible when I was young.

- ☐ I am thankful that I learned the importance of saving money when I was a child.

- ☐ I feel fortunate to have learned as a child how important family is.

_____ I grew up on a farm. My family had to care for the animals morning and evening, seven days a week. Even during school vacations and on weekends, there was work to be done, and each of my brothers and sisters had jobs that our parents depended on us to do.

For example, when I was 12, my parents entrusted me with the care of the young animals. That meant that if an animal was sick or injured, I had to take charge, giving the animal its medication and generally making sure it had a chance to get well. Most farmers had problems with their calves frequently getting sick. I was proud that my calves were usually healthy. That fact alone proved to me that I was doing a good job and making the right decisions.

Another way I learned responsibility is that, from the age of 12, I was paid for my work. Because I was working hard for my own money, I learned how to budget and save. When I was 14, I was able to buy a 10-speed bicycle with my savings. And because I demonstrated how responsible I was, by the time I was 16, my parents trusted me enough to help with the farm accounts.

In conclusion, being allowed to make important decisions and take charge of my own finances at an early age taught me what being responsible really means. Now, in my working life, I know that if I take care of the jobs that are given to me, my colleagues will see they can trust me with even more challenging tasks in the future.

B Now write a composition about something you learned as a child that is useful to you now. Begin the paragraphs as indicated below.

I'm glad that I learned _____

_____

_____

For example, _____

_____

_____

Another way I learned _____

_____

_____

In conclusion, _____

_____

_____

GRAMMAR

Complete the sentences with the correct form of the verbs in parentheses.

1.   Jay: I'm taking a French class at the community college.

     Meryl: I wish I _____*had*_____ (have) more time to learn a second language.

2.   Diego: I have to study tonight.

      Jim: If you _____ (study) yesterday, you would have been able to
             go to the concert with me tonight!

3. Camila: If only our neighbor _____ (play) his music more softly at night!

     Derek: I know. I haven't had a good night's sleep since he moved in!

4.   Rohan: Our boss is going to be upset when he sees what you've done.

     Julie: It's true. If I had been careful, I _____ (not spill) my drink on
             my computer.

5.   Albin: You look exhausted. Why don't you stop working for a few minutes?

      Lily: I wish I _____ (take) a break, but I have too much to do!

6. Hiroto: I'm so glad you didn't get caught in that snowstorm!

      Kay: If you _____ (not warn) me, I probably would have gotten
             stuck on the road.

 GRAMMAR

Complete the sentences with wishes and regrets about the illustration.
Use the phrases from the box.

forget my umbrella	check the weather forecast
wear my raincoat	find a taxi

1. I wish *I hadn't forgotten my umbrella.*
   _____

2. If only _____
   _____

3. I wish _____
   _____

4. If only _____
   _____

3 VOCABULARY

Use the words in the box to complete the sentences.

compassionate	generous	resilient	selfish
discreet	indifference	respect	tolerance

1. Even though Mr. Soto gave a _____*generous*_____ donation to the library fund, he wishes he could have given more.

2. If I had been more _____, Jenny wouldn't have found out about her surprise birthday party.

3. Make sure to be on time for your appointment with Ms. Benson. She doesn't have much _____ for lateness.

4. We lost all _____ for Ben when he lied about what happened to the computer.

5. I think it's important to teach children to be _____ toward others.

6. Gina is pretty _____. Even though she lost the singing competition, she'll be ready to sing again tomorrow.

7. _____ to global warming really bothers me.

8. Brad is so _____. He only thinks about how things affect him.

4 GRAMMAR

Read each situation. Then write one sentence with a wish about the present or future and one sentence with a regret about the past.

1. Tim stopped at a store to get a soda. He put his wallet down on the counter. When he went to pick it up, the wallet was gone! His ID and credit cards were in the wallet.
   Tim wishes he could find his wallet.
   If Tim hadn't set his wallet down, he wouldn't have lost his credit cards.

2. Laura had a 5:00 flight. She planned to take the 3:45 bus to the airport. Unfortunately, the bus was late. She missed her flight.
   _____
   _____

3. Charles was planning to study for four hours for his driver's test the next day. He went to the movies with his friend instead and studied for only 20 minutes. He failed the test.
   _____
   _____

4. Maxine quit going to college in her junior year. She planned to take one year off to travel and then go back to school. That was five years ago.
   _____
   _____

A Read the article quickly. Decades ago, what was the assumption about how the Internet would affect people's honesty?

Internet On, Inhibitions Off:
Why We Tell All On The Net

It is now well known that people are generally accurate and (sometimes embarrassingly) honest about their personalities when profiling themselves on social networking sites. Patients are willing to be more open about psychiatric symptoms to an automated online doctor than a real one. Pollsters find that people give more honest answers to an online survey than to one conducted by phone.

But online honesty cuts both ways. Bloggers find that readers who comment on their posts are often harshly frank, but that these same rude critics become polite if contacted directly. . . .

Why is this? Why do we become more honest the less we have to face each other? Posing the question may make the answer seem obvious – that we feel uncomfortable about confessing to or challenging others when face to face with them – but that begs the question: Why? This is one of those cases where it is helpful to compare human beings with other species, to set our behavior in context.

In many monkeys and apes, face-to-face contact is essentially antagonistic. Staring is a threat. . . . Put two monkey strangers in a cage and they keep well apart, avoid eye contact, and generally do their utmost to avoid triggering a fight. Put two people in an elevator and the same thing happens. . . .

For many primates, face-to-face contact carries a threat. When we're online, we're essentially faceless. Deep in our psyches, the act of writing a furious online critique of someone's views does not feel like a confrontation, whereas telling them the same thing over the phone or face to face does. All the cues are missing that would warn us not to risk a revenge attack by being too frank. . . .

Internet flaming and its benign equivalent, online honesty, are a surprise. Two decades ago, most people thought the anonymity of the online world would cause an epidemic of dishonesty, just as they thought it would lead to geeky social isolation. Then along came social networking, and the Internet not only turned social but became embarrassingly honest. . . .

B Read the article again. Choose the correct answers.

1. What do social networking sites and automated online doctors have in common?
   - ☐ a. They make people more honest.
   - ☐ b. They make people less trustworthy.
   - ☐ c. They make people more ethical.

2. A monkey that stands face-to-face with another monkey probably . . .
   - ☐ a. wants to be agreeable.
   - ☐ b. is showing respect.
   - ☐ c. is looking for a fight.

3. Why does the writer talk about monkeys and apes in the article?
   - ☐ a. To make a contrast with human behavior.
   - ☐ b. To help explain human behavior.
   - ☐ c. To point out animals are capable of dishonesty.

4. What does the author suggest is the cause of online frankness?
   - ☐ a. People have become less sociable.
   - ☐ b. It's human nature to confront others.
   - ☐ c. We don't feel threatened for saying what we think.

1 GRAMMAR

Look at the timeline that a mother has envisioned for her twins' lives. Are the sentences true or false? Choose the correct answer. Then rewrite the false sentences to make them true.

Max and Ava's Timeline

January 2010
born

September 2015
go to school for the first time

June 2032
graduate from college

August 2032
leave on a trip around the world

July 2035
return home from trip

October 2035
start their careers

	True	False
1. By September 2026, Max and Ava will have been going to school for 10 years.	☐	☑

By September 2026, Max and Ava will have been going to school for 11 years.

	True	False
2. By July 2032, they will already have graduated from college.	☐	☐
3. By September 2033, they will be leaving on a trip around the world.	☐	☐
4. By August 2035, they will have been traveling for three years.	☐	☐
5. It's now October 2034. By this time next year, they will have started their careers.	☐	☐
6. By October 2037, they will have been working for one year.	☐	☐

2 GRAMMAR

Complete the email. Use the future perfect
or future perfect continuous of the verbs
in parentheses.

To: Julie
Cc:
Subject: Paris!

Hi Julie,

By this time tomorrow, I (1) _____**will have arrived**_____ (arrive) in France! I can't believe I get to
study there! I'm nervous, but I hope by next week I (2) _____ (learn) my
way around. I'm sure I (3) _____ (get) lost several times by then, too.

I (4) _____ (meet) my roommate by this time next week, too. I hope she's
nice. I'm nervous about meeting my new classmates. They're all from different parts of the world.
I hope in six month's time I (5) _____ (have) the opportunity to get to
know each of them.

I can't wait for you to visit. Maybe you can come in December. That should give you some time to
save money since you (6) _____ (work) for a few months by then. And
also by then, I'm sure I (7) _____ (find) some great restaurants to eat at. I
know how much you love French food!

I already miss you, so write to me as soon as you can!

Isabella

3 VOCABULARY

Complete the sentences with *about, in, of, to,* or *with*. Sometimes more than
one answer is possible.

1. Kenji can't wait for his trip to the United States. He's looking forward _____**to**_____
   visiting California and New York.

2. Before Nicole left to work in her company's branch in Spain, she participated
   _____ a special training program.

3. If you have the opportunity to work in another country, don't be scared _____
   taking it.

4. Michelle made friends easily after she adjusted _____ the new culture.

5. Jack was very excited _____ meeting his colleagues from China.

6. If you want to take advantage _____ your school's study abroad programs,
   you should talk to your adviser.

7. She wasn't familiar _____ the customs in her host country, but she
   soon adapted to life there.

8. As soon as he became aware _____ his company's policy allowing employees
   to work in another country for a year, he decided to apply.

WRITING

A Read the three conclusions about the experience of working abroad. Write the letters of all the methods used in each conclusion.

a. looks to the future   c. summarizes the main points
b. concludes with the main idea d. makes recommendations

_b, c, d_ 1. In conclusion, those who decide to live abroad gain experience of other cultures, understanding of others' work practices, and a deeper empathy for people of other countries. Working abroad widens your view of the world, and that will be of lasting benefit in both your work and personal life. Definitely do it if you can.

_____ 2. To sum up, people who decide to work abroad will have the opportunity to change their lives in several ways. First, they will develop a deep understanding of another culture. Second, they will gain first-hand experience of work practices that can give them a new perspective on their own work. Last, they will broaden their knowledge of the world in ways that will stay with them for the rest of their lives.

_____ 3. In brief, whether you decide to work abroad on a short-term basis or for an extended period, it is an experience that is educational, pleasurable, and practical. The experience allows you to flourish in all aspects of your life long after the experience is over and is highly recommended for anyone who has the chance to do it.

B Underline the words or phrases in each conclusion above that helped you decide which methods were used.

C Write a short essay about what people should expect to experience if they come to work or study in your country. Your conclusion should contain at least one of the methods listed above.

_____
_____
_____
_____
_____
_____
_____
_____
_____
_____
_____
_____
_____
_____
_____
_____
_____
_____

1 GRAMMAR

Use the verbs in parentheses to complete the email. Use mixed conditionals.

Dear Elena,

Well, I'm halfway through my tour of Peru. I'd like to say that everything is going well, but unfortunately, that isn't the case. I think if I (1) ____*had prepared*____ (prepare) a little more thoroughly, I (2) _____ (enjoy) myself a lot more right now. I guess if I (3) _____ (take) more time to research where I was going to stay, I (4) _____ (have) a better time in this beautiful country.

My biggest mistake is that I didn't bring the right clothes. I brought all my summer clothes, and it is absolutely freezing! If I (5) _____ (bring) the right clothes, I (6) _____ (feel) more comfortable right now. Instead, I've been staying indoors as much as possible and have a terrible cold. I went to a local pharmacy to get some cold medicine, but I had some trouble reading the labels. I think I bought the wrong medicine. If I (7) _____ (buy) the right medicine, I (8) _____ (not sneeze) all the time! If I (9) _____ (follow) your advice about the weather and accommodations, I (10)_____ (not have) so many problems right now!

Anyway, I'll remember next time.
I miss you!

Love,
Sophia
Attached: perutrip014.jpg

2 GRAMMAR

Match the clauses to make conditional sentences. Write the correct letter.

1. If I had packed more carefully, _____
2. If I hadn't chosen a discount airline, _____
3. If I had studied English more often, _____
4. If I had left for the airport earlier, _____
5. If I hadn't forgotten my novel, _____

a. I wouldn't be afraid to ask people for directions.
b. I wouldn't be reading a boring magazine right now.
c. I wouldn't be searching my bags for my passport.
d. I would have a free movie to look forward to on board.
e. I wouldn't be worried about missing my flight!

3 VOCABULARY

What characteristics do you think would be most important for these people?
Write sentences about each picture using the adjectives from the box.

culturally aware	nonconforming	open-minded	self-motivated
culturally sensitive	nonjudgmental	self-assured	self-reliant

mountain climber

businessperson abroad

1. The mountain climber has to be ____*self-reliant*____ because *she could be left*
   *on her own in an emergency.*_____

2. If the mountain climber weren't _____, she _____
   _____

3. The businessperson abroad should be _____
   _____

4. If the businessperson abroad weren't _____
   _____

4 GRAMMAR

Complete the sentences so they are true for you.

1. If I had been open-minded about *studying abroad in college, I would have*
   *much more international experience on my résumé.*_____

2. If I had been more self-assured when _____,
   I _____

3. If I had been more culturally aware when I was younger, I _____
   _____

4. If I hadn't been open-minded about _____,
   I _____

A Read the article quickly. Choose the tips that are mentioned.

☐ call your friends at home   ☐ spend a lot of time alone

☐ take a course in anthropology   ☐ prepare for culture shock

☐ take a class for people going abroad   ☐ visit a doctor regularly

BEATING CULTURE SHOCK

You have a chance to live and work overseas, to get to know another culture from the inside. It's a wonderful opportunity, but don't be surprised if you experience at least some culture shock. "When you're put into a new culture, even simple things will throw you. You become like a child again, unable to handle everyday life without help," says L. Robert Kohls, an expert on culture shock.

Taking an intercultural studies or anthropology course at a university or attending one of the many classes offered for people going abroad is an important way to reduce the stress of culture shock, says Elsie Purnell, the founder of a counseling agency. She advises people going overseas to expect culture shock and to try to be prepared for it.

Someone living in a new culture typically goes through four stages of adjustment. Initial euphoria, or the honeymoon stage, is characterized by high expectations, a focus on similarities in the new culture, and a tendency to attach positive values to any differences that are noticed.

Culture shock, the second stage, begins very suddenly. The symptoms of culture shock include homesickness, feelings of anxiety, depression, fatigue, and inadequacy. Some people going through culture shock try to withdraw from the new culture, spending most of their free time reading about home, sleeping 12 hours a night, and associating only with others from their own country. Others eat too much, feel irritable, and display hostility or even aggression.

A period of gradual adjustment is the third stage. Once you realize you're adjusting, life gets more hopeful. "You've been watching what's been going on, interpreting things, and you're starting to recognize the patterns and learn the underlying values of the culture," says Kohls. It feels more natural, and you feel more self-assured.

The fourth stage, full adjustment, can take several years, and not everyone achieves it. According to Kohls, a lot depends on people's personalities – how rigid or how easygoing they are – and how seriously they try to understand the new culture.

B Read the article again. At what stage would someone make the following statements?

	Stage 1	Stage 2	Stage 3	Stage 4
1. "I just want to sleep all the time."	☐	☑	☐	☐
2. "The customs here are different, but they are so wonderful and sophisticated!"	☐	☐	☐	☐
3. "I've lived here for so many years that it feels like home."	☐	☐	☐	☐
4. "Everyone has been so helpful and friendly since I've arrived. The people here are so polite!"	☐	☐	☐	☐
5. "I'm starting to understand the culture and feel more self-assured here."	☐	☐	☐	☐
6. "I only spend time with people from my own country."	☐	☐	☐	☐